SCHIRMER'S LIBRARY OF MUSICAL CLASSICS

Vol. 2119

THE BAROQUE ERA PIANO ALBUM

80 Favorite Pieces by

J.S. Bach

Couperin

Handel

Purcell

Scarlatti

ISBN 978-1-4950-5162-3

G. SCHIRMER, Inc.

DISTRIBUTED BY

HAL•LEONARD®

www.halleonard.com

Contact us:
Hal Leonard
7777 West Bluemound Road
Milwaukee, WI 53213
Email: info@halleonard.com

In Europe, contact:
Hal Leonard Europe Limited
42 Wigmore Street
Marylebone, London, W1U 2RN
Email: info@halleonardeurope.com

In Australia, contact:
Hal Leonard Australia Pty. Ltd.
4 Lentara Court
Cheltenham, Victoria, 3192 Australia
Email: info@halleonard.com.au

CONTENTS

ITALIAN CONCERTO
in F Major

I.

Johann Sebastian Bach
BWV 971

II.

III.

SARABANDE
from English Suite No. 5 in E minor

Johann Sebastian Bach
BWV 810

FRENCH SUITE NO. 2

in C minor

Johann Sebastian Bach
BWV 813

Allemande
Allegro moderato (♩ = 80)

Courante
Vivace ($\flat\cdot = 76$)

26

Sarabande
Andantino (♩ = 84)

Air
Un poco Andante (♩=80)

Menuet
Allegretto (♩ = 120)

Gigue
Allegro (♩. = 88)

FRENCH SUITE NO. 3

in B minor

Johann Sebastian Bach
BWV 814

Allemande

Allegro moderato (♩ = 92)

Courante
Allegro vivace (♩.=66)

Sarabande
Andantino (♩=80)

Menuet I
Con moto moderato (♩=120)

Menuet II
(Trio)

Men. I. da Capo.

Anglaise

Vivace (♩=104)

Gigue
Allegro (♩.=84)

RONDEAU
from Partita No. 2 in C minor

Johann Sebastian Bach
BWV 826

INVENTION NO. 1

in C Major

Johann Sebastian Bach
BWV 772

INVENTION NO. 2

in C minor

Johann Sebastian Bach
BWV 773

INVENTION NO. 4

in D minor

Johann Sebastian Bach
BWV 775

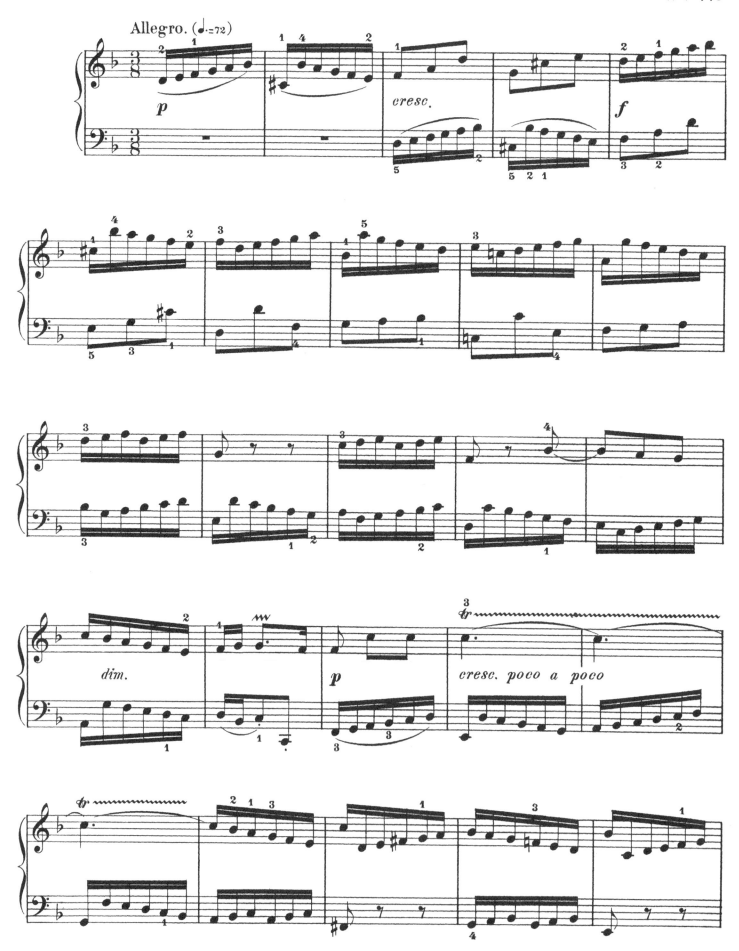

INVENTION NO. 8

in F Major

Johann Sebastian Bach

BWV 779

INVENTION NO. 13

in A minor

Johann Sebastian Bach
BWV 784

PRELUDE NO. 1

in C Major

from *The Well-Tempered Clavier*, Book I

Johann Sebastian Bach
BWV 846

FUGUE NO. 1

in C Major

from *The Well-Tempered Clavier*, Book I

Johann Sebastian Bach

BWV 846

PRELUDE NO. 2

in C minor

from *The Well-Tempered Clavier*, Book I

Johann Sebastian Bach

BWV 847

Allegro vivace (♩ = 144)

FUGUE NO. 2

in C minor

from *The Well-Tempered Clavier*, Book I

Johann Sebastian Bach

BWV 847

PRELUDE IN D MINOR

Johann Sebastian Bach

BWV 899

PRELUDE IN C MAJOR

Johann Sebastian Bach
BWV 924

PRELUDE IN G MAJOR

Johann Sebastian Bach
BWV 902a

PRELUDE IN C MAJOR

(original D Major)

Johann Sebastian Bach
BWV 925

PRELUDE IN D MINOR

Johann Sebastian Bach
BWV 926

Moderato tranquillo

PRELUDE IN B-FLAT MAJOR

(original C Major)

Johann Sebastian Bach
BWV 933

PRELUDE IN D MAJOR

Johann Sebastian Bach
BWV 936

PRELUDE IN E MINOR

Johann Sebastian Bach
BWV 938

PRELUDE IN C MAJOR

Johann Sebastian Bach
BWV 939

PRELUDE IN C MINOR

Johann Sebastian Bach
BWV 999

ARIA DA CAPO
in G Major
from *Goldberg Variations*

Johann Sebastian Bach
BWV 988

LA BANDOLINE

Rondeau

from *Premier livre de pièces de clavecin*

François Couperin

Leggero, senza allegrezza.
Légèrement, sans vitesse.

* May be omitted.

LES BARRICADES MYSTÉRIEUSES

Rondeau

from *Premier livre de pièces de clavecin*

François Couperin

LES PAPILLONS

from *Premier livre de pièces de clavecin*

François Couperin

★ All mordents may be omitted.

SŒUR MONIQUE

from *Premier livre de pièces de clavecin*

François Couperin

★ May be omitted.

a) original

b) original

SUITE IN C MINOR

La Ténébreuse

François Couperin

Courante.

La Lugubre

Sarabande.
Lento.

Gavotte.

AIR

The Harmonious Blacksmith
from Suite in E Major

George Frideric Handel
HWV 430

Double III.
Vivace.

Double IV.
L'istesso tempo.

a) opp:

Double V.
Sempre Vivace.

PRELUDE
from Suite in E Major

George Frideric Handel
HWV 430

COURANTE
from Suite in G Major

George Frideric Handel
HWV 441

AIR
from Suite in D minor

George Frideric Handel
HWV 436

SARABANDE
from Suite in D minor

George Frideric Handel
HWV 437

AIR

from Suite in B-flat Major

George Frideric Handel
HWV 434

Var. V.

ALLEGRO
from Suite in G minor

George Frideric Handel
HWV 432

GIGUE
from Suite in E minor

George Frideric Handel
HWV 429

Vivace.

SARABANDE
from Suite in E minor

George Frideric Handel
HWV 429

la 2da volta ritardando.

SUITE NO. 7
in D minor

Henry Purcell
Z. 668

Almand.
Molto moderato.

Courante.

Moderato.

Hornpipe.

SUITE NO. 2
in G minor

Henry Purcell
Z. 661

Prelude.
Allegro.

★ = omit.

Almand.
Moderato.

Courante.
Andante.

Saraband.
Sostenuto.

a) or ⅃⅃⅃ b) or ⅃⅃⅃

Chacone.

Animato. (♩ = 108)

Siciliano.

SONATA IN A MINOR

Domenico Scarlatti
K. 3, L. 378, P. 59

SONATA IN A MINOR

Domenico Scarlatti
K. 7, L. 373, P. 63

SONATA IN C MINOR

Domenico Scarlatti
K. 84, L. 10, P. 45

SONATA IN C MINOR

Domenico Scarlatti
K. 116, L. 452, P. 111

SONATA IN D MAJOR

Domenico Scarlatti
K. 119, L. 415, P. 217

Tremulo nell' A la mi re

SONATA IN A MAJOR

Domenico Scarlatti
K. 208, L. 238, P. 315

Andante e cantabile

SONATA IN G MAJOR

Domenico Scarlatti
K. 260, L. 124, P. 304

97

107

116

125

134

143

SONATA IN E MINOR

Domenico Scarlatti
K. 263, L. 321, P. 283

SONATA IN E MAJOR

Domenico Scarlatti
K. 264, L. 466, P. 308

SONATA IN C MAJOR

Domenico Scarlatti
K. 309, L. 454, P. 333

Allegro

52

57

62

67

72

SONATA IN F MAJOR

Domenico Scarlatti
K. 366, L. 119, P. 263

158

SONATA IN C MAJOR

Domenico Scarlatti
K. 420, L. S2, P. 352

SONATA IN C MAJOR

Domenico Scarlatti
K. 421, L. 252, P. 459

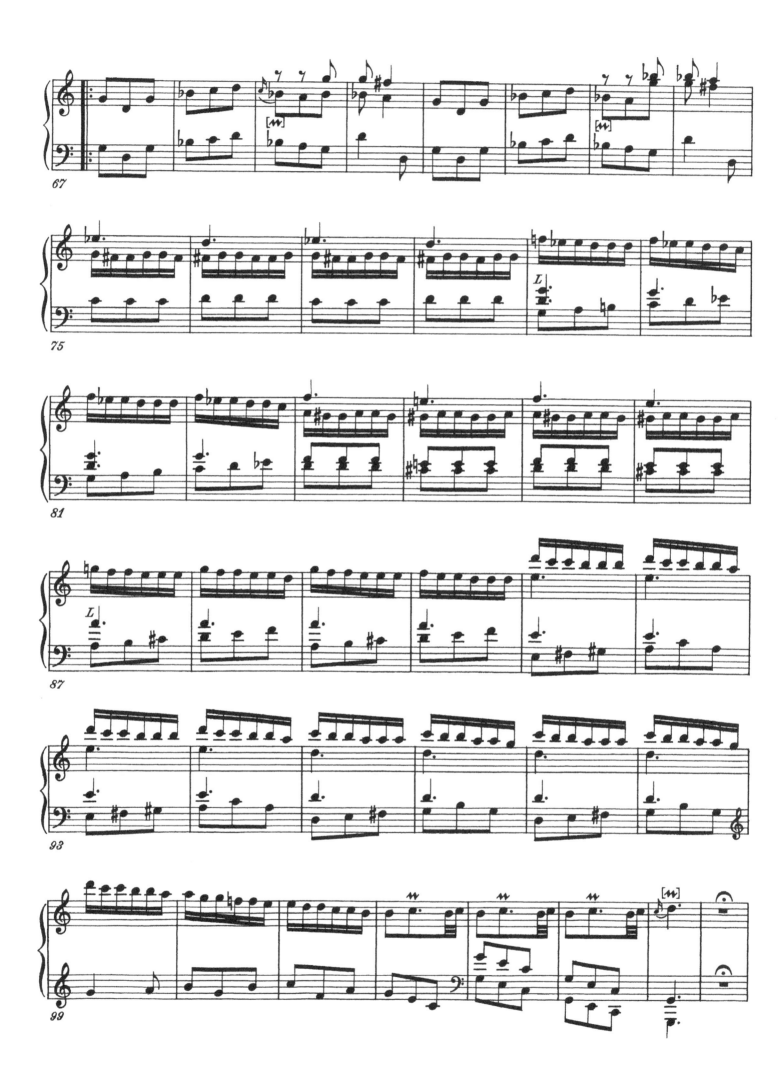

SONATA IN G MAJOR

Domenico Scarlatti
K. 427, L. 286, P. 286

SONATA IN D MINOR

Domenico Scarlatti
K. 517, L. 266, P. 517

SONATA IN B-FLAT MAJOR

Domenico Scarlatti
K. 544, L. 497, P. 548

175